HE COMES RUNNING

HE COMES RUNNING

A Turkish Sojourn

&

Myths We Never Knew

Daniel Abdal-Hayy Moore

The Ecstatic Exchange
2014
Philadelphia

For quotes any longer than those for critical articles and reviews,
contact:
The Ecstatic Exchange,
6470 Morris Park Road, Philadelphia, PA 19151-2403
email: abdalhayy@danielmoorepoetry.com

First Edition
ISBN: 978-0-578-13792-6 (paper)
Published by *The Ecstatic Exchange,*
6470 Morris Park Road, Philadelphia, PA 19151-2403

Cover and all calligraphy by Haji Noor Deen Mi Guang Jiang
Book design by the author
Back cover photographs © Peter Sanders

بسم الله الرحمن الرحيم

DEDICATION

To

Shaykh ibn al-Habib

(and the continuation of the Habibiyya)

Shaykh Bawa Muhaiyuddeen,

all shuyukh of instruction and ma'arifa,

our hosts Faruk Dilaver, Musa Levin

and the Turkish dervishes

&

Baji Tayyaba Khanum

of the unsounded depths

*

The earth is not bereft
of Light

INTRODUCTION

Turkey is a place I might not have visited, having entered Sufic Islam via the Habibiyya Tariqa of Shaykh Muhammad ibn al-Habib (*rahimahu'llah*) in 1970, and through various visits to the great awliya of Morocco and Algeria, finding my spiritual center aligned most resonantly with the ways, practices and illuminations of North Africa. But we were all reading Arberry's translation of *The Discourses of Rumi* in the 60s in Berkeley, and when I bought the Nicholson volumes of Rumi's *Mathnawi* at Shambala Bookstore on Telegraph Avenue, I knew I'd found the apex of possible spiritual poetry, a notion that has only deepened with time. So behind everything has always been a connection, not uncommon it's true, with Mevlana Rumi as poet, teacher and saint.

So with an invitation at the beginning of May, 2002, to visit a modern exponent of the Turkish way, Faruk Dilaver, through poet/saint Yunus Emre, and Rumi's mode of thought and indirect instruction, I accompanied a group of wayfarers there. In their honor, I made an intention to record my visit with poems in strict *ghazal* form, resulting in *The Flame of Transformation Turns to Light, Ninety-Nine Ghazals Written in English*. A number of them record the lightningbolt embrace and its aftermath I felt upon entering Rumi's tomb in Konya, having so anticipated the visit from Berkeley on.

A second visit, again to meet and sit with Faruk Abi, in September of 2003, resulted in the book of poems, *Love is a Letter Burning in a High Wind*, with its favorite opening poem, *On the Road to Konya*, and a number of poems written in and off Rumi's tomb itself, as well as in the nearby memorial tomb of Shams, and others written during our travels to such places as Capadoccia.

Then most recently, in November of 2013, my wife Malika and I were invited to accompany dear friends to Istanbul, where Faruk would be visiting many of his Yunus Emre circle in people's houses (with often lavish dinners and décor) and listen long into the night to his *sohbets*, or talks, attended by wall to wall beloveds hanging on his every word, filled with wonderful and passionate zeal. Not knowing any Turksh, and many of the "translators" knowing only a curious English, with some superb exceptions, I found myself inspired to write poems from the prevailing atmosphere of such open-ended and deep spirituality.

Early in our stay, and after a tour of Istanbul's magnificent mosques, we went to lunch, where I noticed a tray of cut papers (6X4 inches in fact) by a telephone, for taking notes, easily fit in the pocket — a little pile of which I availed myself. Then one evening of talks I took out a page and wrote the first of what would result in this chronological series of poems written over the period of our two-week stay, intentionally keeping to only one poem per page, in free form not as formal but perhaps as stringently limiting as the *ghazals* from my first visit. Something ignited, the forced brevity, the nights of hearing various decipherments of the Turkish, snatches and bits of the sweet and sometimes fierce wisdom from Faruk, the strong love in the air — as well as from some of the other trips we took, the Black Sea, the markets, etc. I ended up with the fifty short poems I now present, each here on their own page, line by line as they were written. Hopefully they focus heartfelt fragments of The Path to Allah, love of His Prophet Muhammad, *salallahu alayhi wa sallam*, and His living sages, those physically present and those absent, with us in God's creation until the end of time.

(The additional poems, Myths We Never Knew, *were written during the same sojourn directly onto my iPad, a kind of experiment unusual for me who always writes in notebooks in longhand, with pen.)*

February, 13, 2014

Allah says: "I am as My servant expects Me to be,
and I am with him when he remembers Me.
If he thinks of Me, I think of him.
If he mentions Me in company,
I mention him in even better company.
When he comes closer to Me by a handspan,
I come closer to him by an arm's length.
If he draws closer to Me by an arm's length,
I draw closer by a distance of two outstretched arms
nearer to him.
If my Servant comes to me walking,
I go to him running."

Hadith Qudsi — Al-Bukhari

"Multiply yourself by zero."

— Baji Tayyaba Khanum

1

The exercise of diminishment
increases to a zero in which
all the flowers of the sacred
send out aromatic pods and
leaves of the Ninety-Nine
Names of God

If the five elements intrude
fold each one inside the other
on the great angelic wheel
that slices into the
Magnetic Mountain
in the space of no space
and swallow its drops into a
heart free of both earth and
heaven

2

If you destroy a portion of the good
increase in zones of generosity

and the sharp dragon's tail will
shrivel to lizard length
and soon disappear under a leaf

———————————————

Mannequins in God's fancy shops
could be said to be facing

eternity or simply turning their
rigid backs on the world

As they maintain absolute silence
we can only speculate on their

sincerity or wonder if they
in fact know more than we do

3

A little bowl of spinach
across from the leather shop
carries with it odors of a
greener world than this one
even as it comes from the
greenness of this one

Fresh spring water right off
the busy street carries within it
rainbows from the spray of
waterfalls crossing each other
in paradisiacal arcs

If you see a face looking
back at you your surprise
is nothing compared to its

as the spray water dissolves
the outlines of both

4

Overhead lights don't
exist in gypsy camps that aren't
stars in decipherable
constellations whose illumined
walls are traversed by centaurs
and roaring lions

Reflections on marble don't
exist in deserts whose baked
dunes change places with
mirages of cities lost in the
sophistications of their deaths
as their gates close for
the night

Real walls tumble down
as real trees grow tall
and sway in real wind

5

Has the cloud of love hovered
over the countries of death?
Are blasted house fronts and
crumbled doors signs of love
gone sour? Have the people
run wild through streets
in search of God's love or in
flight from it? Is its Light
too bright to bear? Are even
sips of it too much for some?

Will we all sizzle down to a
regular surf at last at love's
ocean's edge to endure its
delirious intensities? A dark
sky slashed from end to
end in light?

Muhammad Rasulullah

Muhammad, Prophet of Allah

peace and blessings of Allah be upon him,

(in the shape of his blessed sandal)

6

Lungs are cutting through forests
of cigarette smoke in close
quarters with windows
shut tight

No relief in sight

Breath in short intakes to
filter what smoke can be
filtered but certain vipers
seem to thrive on it and
grow longer and stronger
as we shrink and become
weaker

Will the windows to let in
fresh air never be opened?

7

A rolling road slowly rises
out of dark blue cloud

Various figures can be seen
moving slowly to and fro
inside the cloud as they find a
way to the road to begin a
long trek out
though their equipment be
frail and in deep need of repair
before they attempt it and the
road rise suddenly
at a steep angle upward

Carry the papers and the
stick given you and an
owl's scrutiny and a
cougar's stealth

8

A king is coming

Not the king of a country but
a king of himself and a
vastness inside his kingdom of self
for the One King to reside and
flow through to the empty
kingdoms outside himself where
the One King also resides whether
or not they know and lay
waste to the night-crawlers
who lay in wait to waylay those
waiting for the One King to
arrive

A king is coming

He will arrive soon and
everything will change

9

Sometimes the King comes and
sometimes the circus comes
and they both occupy the
same tent surrounded by
tame lions and clowns

Sunlight after a day of rain
can show us which is which

I saw a flock of crows
and a flock of geese

The crows were having a
powwow in the treetops

The geese were following their
leader in the sky south for
the winter glittering with
wintry light

10

The nearby dogs are silent
the distant dogs still bark

This is only some of the things you can
pick out in the dark

A bridge of flame is falling
the night sky fills a glass

the earth is trembling in
expectation of what will come to pass

The captain of the ship
has long gone down below

Only God can steer us to
safety now before we'll have to row

11

At the dawn call to prayer from
the nearby lovely spindly-minareted
mosque crossing adhans from other
minarets by loudspeakers all the
dogs near and far begin to yip and
howl and bark in chorus as well

Are they Satan's dogs howling in
disrespect to keep the believers
away or are they God's dogs
joyously celebrating the calls
and joining in annunciatory glee

extending the call to the dog
world and any other sleepy
canines within the ears' both
short and triangular or long and floppy
compass of sound?

12

There were chickens and geese
and strange pointy goose-tongues as
they hacked their greetings or
admonitions at us through the
fence

Then later sheep and straggly
odorless rose bushes and a
bright orange flower with
sheep in the distance

A bare and barren landscape
with dry grasses rough hedges and
bluish mountains in the distance
that Van Gogh with bamboo pens
and sepia and India ink could
bring to vibrant life with quick
stipple strokes and a thousand
heartfelt dots

13

While awaiting the king's arrival
seventy foals were born in
a barn filled with illuminated
straw

Three cities submitted to a very
short tyrant's army because of
the size of the brass buttons on
their uniforms

Hair and nails got longer and the
seasons changed

Little by little a fair outline of the
king emerged and some said
they saw it between the forest
trees and others that they ate
with it just after dawn

Maybe the king was already
with us all along

14

In a well-appointed room
with multiple conversations
the children's footsteps could be
heard above them on the wooden
floors

Swans floated on the word
streams and some ducks
also slept with their heads
tucked under their wings

Echoes intruded and had their
own opinions but few paid
them the attention they were
due

Voices rose and fell
Doors opened and closed

No one moved in the lexicons
of the air

15

When the horses came through
the landscapes they came through
flowed from their manes

In their eyes we saw the vision
of Allah they saw and wept

Large brown pools and every
phase of the moon in an
instant stretched from the
first to the last eternity
and back again in a moment
hanging from the eyelashes of
landscapes that had become
horses in leafy motion as
stationary as trees

Only Allah sees Allah
and only He knows Himself

Everything else is air and water

16

When he spoke in a language
only some of us knew there was
a screen of lights and shadows
and unseen flights of meaning
seeking their sources
in the hearts inside our ears
and ears inside our
hearts

But no one could repeat
word for word what he said

And waters of a golden
comprehension rose above
our knees that know
prostration and our foreheads
that practice submission

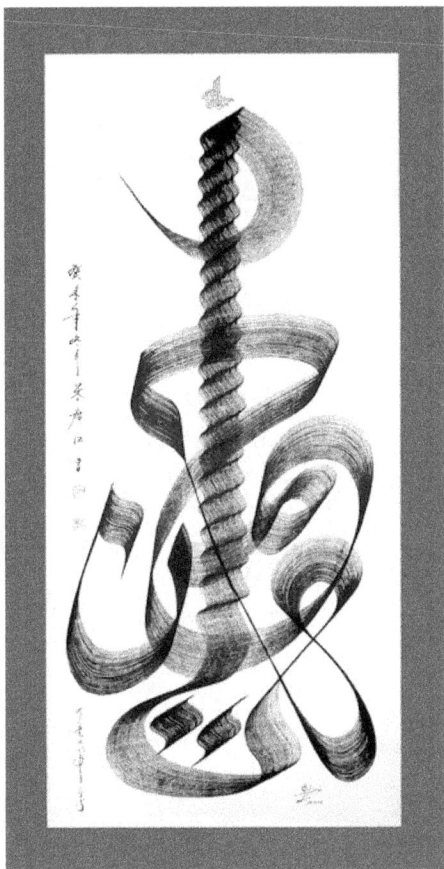

17

To die before you die is to find
a meaning that stays meaning
that when north becomes south
and west becomes east meaning
stays in its high crystal
receiving the light it emits

When we become beside ourselves
we become most and nothing at
one stroke

If we step out of one space in
our original shape the showers
of His Mercy descend and fill
the space of all emptiness until
nothing is left and everything is
just as it is in Allah's Grace

18

At the stroke of One
His Mercy began

At the stroke of two the
world was full

At the stroke of three
space gleamed

At the stroke of four
all looseness tightened

And at the stroke of five
a stream of bees visited the
lips of the Beloved to spread
His sweetness through the
creation and let its drops
drip into our hearts

Numbers dissolved into essences
and essences dissolved into
all of us at once again

19

How can He be otherwise
than where we are?

Hearing news of Him was the
end of knowledge of Him

We began unreeling this thread
and will end by reeling it in
again and the end is in the
beginning and its end and
beginning and span between
are from Him Who is only
where we are and whose
only "where" is where we are

It is a hollow thread and
shines

And is a Voice more than a
thread and a shattering of
Light in secret places

20

We have come here to be
where He is

Hello to distance
Be in our hearts!

Hello to the winds of where we
are

Take us to Him Who is where we
are

Tell Him we are here to be
where He is which is where
we are

If there was anywhere where
He wasn't there would be
nowhere where He is

But that is not possible
so He is Here

21

In the sweet aftermath
dogs bark and a rooster crows
his hens around him meekly
pecking the ground

And night drapes her long
gowns over the world and
fastens them with the moon's
crescent

Has the king's robe caught on a
chair leg as he passed by?
Has a fluff of his ermine fallen
from his robe onto our Path?

Is the air around our bodies and
in our lungs the same?

Mirrors have shifted and fallen
into their silver backings to
reveal the rose garden they
always were
in sunlit shafts

22

Since I couldn't understand what
he was saying I decided to
write down what he said

At this the geese who had
honked at us in the afternoon
took flight in distinct and
elegant formations until
the skies were white with
them

Not knowing his words I
listened for their echoes and
found the well they were
emitting from not far from
where I was and was
not

An authenticating seal floated down
like a goose feather and stamped its
circle of light here

23

When love drives a furrow
through death's pasture the
only crop that grows
is lovers

Don't tell me sunlight and rain
don't reach these fields or
that black crows with the
knives and forks of their beaks
will gobble up the seeds and
leave it fallow

Even fallow yields results as
one vibration in love's direction
is enough to effect the required
atoms for all good to grow

"He comes running"

Even from the farthest dry
outpost or the seeming-most
bare and piebald station
death-mound vacancy

24

Oh son of the beloved
stand in the center of this walking
though I only caught a few
rare glimpses of your face
always hooded in God-Snow
and God-Light at the far end
where you started down the hill

You left your inviolable impression
in the air no one dares enter
but from which all may draw
any treasure they can whether of
glass or silence or the dance of
shadows against a wall

Even in broad daylight and the
sun directly overhead your
light is greater by God

No one can forget the sound of
horses cantering away

25

The king sits under any tree and
on any rock in any windblown
landscape on earth or heaven
to converse with crickets and
bluebirds in their daily passages

No subjects escape his notice
though he may not mention them
by name but only elude to
their velvet edges as they age
and wither

He's always news fresh and
alive and up to the moment

His notice is Allah's notice
and each special ant under
his gaze carries the sunlight
of longevity and the moonlight
of death's sugary banquets

26

Heartfelt advice begins in one
and leaps across to another who's
asked in all heartfelt openness

In the air it takes the color of
possible storms and desert
stillnesses in which no fox ear
twitches nor scorpion digs

Will its balm reach the
recipient's bones and enter their
marrow enough to transform
today's tomorrow?

Will buildings in the mind block
the sun or cast longer shadows?

Alleyways behind the elegant
facades of the heart wriggle and
zigzag into out-gates and into
more breathable atmospheres

27

The heart came out of the body
and spoke and by heart we mean
that living forest of swinging birds
and musical knowledges interwoven
among the leaves of ancient trees

By the heart we mean the heart
of the heart which is a boundless
ocean waiting for the touch of God
to illumine under the brightest sky

By heart what is meant is what
already knows the truth the
way trees know to grow

When the singer began to sing a
voice from far away came up
through his throat where many
drunk dervishes have vanished
and reappeared

28

A brave and ruined man
became a sudden flying bird
whose wingspread spanned the
skies

He closed his eyes in a crowded
room and a chorus of voices
trembled through his fluttering
voice that drew water from
invisible wells and spun
honey from invisible hives

Salaams from a shore
beyond water and an ocean
beyond waves

A sky leans down and takes
us by our hands to draw us
up

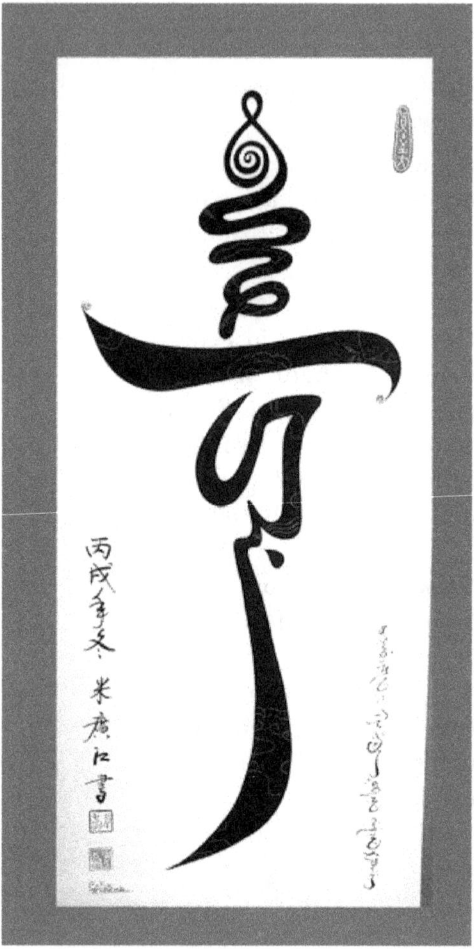
丙戌年冬 米廣江書

29

Sometimes the dawn comes
up so silently you don't notice
that its tissues of gold have
slid over everything with the
just-as-it-is-ness of everything
placid in its light

It's been said a dragon sleeps
in the mountain unkilled and
undefeated although no one's
seen it firsthand except
those who've set out to rid
us of its menace

Some people also disappear
into daylight and are never
seen again

A weak post-dawn crowing of
a rooster can just be heard

30

The peace you see in his
eyes is that he's always happy

The peace you see in his eyes is that
he's always satisfied

The peace you see in his eyes is that he's
always with Allah

If a giant camel came or a small
yellow taxi he'd get on or in it
all the same to go where he
wants and where he wants is Allah

He knows Allah is First and Last
First before firstness and Last
beyond lastness and He is the Outwardly
Manifest and the Inwardly Hidden

The peace in his eyes is the tangerine
he's eating and the tea he's sipping

31

The least fly lands on a
shiny black Mercedes trunk lid
and feels at home

Sunlight expands to all far
corners at once with God's
Name on its chapped lips

Waters keep rushing to
forward places over rocks

Mankind takes a breath
and lets it out again

I think mountains will rip
themselves open out of love for
Allah and plains will
become plainer to shrink
themselves before His Majesty

32

At one point the King drops
everything and emerges from his
separate body as pure spirit

No birds fall out of their trees
but the skies coalesce above him
and hover to watch over his
sudden nakedness

Orchestras in far islands awaken
and sit behind their miraculously
tuned instruments and at a tiny
twig crack begin their heavenly
music

The King keeps going and coming
into and out of himself and
every other self in creation
since he's left his own self
behind

33

Pine nuts come from
little scrubby pine trees with long
dark green needles along the side of the
road

We all come from Allah

Coffee scent from a steaming cup
of coffee can be traced back to
its source set out for us to drink

We can follow traces from our
own obstreperous beings to our
Magnificent and Beauteous Lord

Here's something — sunlight
glittering in an afternoon ride to the
Black Sea diffuses in the air and
igniting our vision everywhere also
can be traced back to the Living
God Life-Giver over all

34

What beasts raise their heads?

What lions in thickets peer through
to watch for movements in the
sun? What gazelles of pure love
whose black pool eyes contain
dark truths of God's Wondrousness
stand too still and vulnerable to
be missed by such patient
leonine scrutiny?

God pounce on me!
Carry me to your lair!

How many earthly breezes and
watery dawns shall I continue
to stand in before I'm taken?

The green oasis shimmers and
the desert stretches around it
to the end of time

35

The King is camped not far
from here in the middle of the
road so that everyone must
acknowledge his existence

For those who have said
the King is not alive they have to
go around a camp of huge pointed
tents of all the hues in the world
and the King's great singers
harmonizing from tent to tent

For those who do know he's with us
there are people in each tent to make
them feel at home with special
banquets and the King visits each
tent personally each night by
special lamplight and gazes into
their eyes with loving gazes

Some go through the camp this
way and others go around but the
King is a patient King
and loves them both

36

If you enter the King's room
there's nothing there
There's only something there when
the King's there

If you take the King away the
nothingness of things without the
King appears

Everything depends on the King

Things may think they can do without
the King and that He appears and
disappears but that's only in the
realm of "things"

He's made it to seem that way
It lets things seem to go their
own way

But their own way that they
don't own is the way with the
King who owns all ways

Everything happens with the King

37

The King couldn't come Himself
or leave His place of origin so He sent
a few messengers of the first rank who
changed the world and many messengers
of the second rank who keep the
machinery running

Everyone knows of the messengers of the
first rank and their names have
interior light in daylight or at
night that illumines the jungle paths

Messengers of the second rank may be
less well-known since many take
menial jobs and may be seen in
unusual places that may even seem
unkingly but their eyes and words
tell the story and their visits
alleviate pain and elevate
hearts

38

There's a black door

Who stands inside the black door?

Who resides within the black door?

Is there a star in the black door?

Do stars come out inside the black
door?

Are all the planets inside the black
door?

It stands here in the blackest of
blackness

It stands open in the blackest of
blackness

It is one door

There is nothing outside it

Outside it there is no blackness

Inside it is a single light

which is everything

39

The lips of the messengers of the
first rank are moving still

The lips of the messengers of the
second rank keep being born

The faces of the messengers of the
first rank rise and enter the
phases of the moon

The faces of the messengers of the
second rank may look out at us
from unexpected places as
common as daylight or as
unique as ecstasy under a
wide and gold-flecked banyan
tree or behind the window of
a shop

But the eyes of the messengers of both
first and second rank are the
same

And their hearts contain only Allah

40

The prophets enter the world from
Allah's Presence
through the black door

The saints enter Allah's Presence
through the black door
from the world

No edges exist from both
directions and the frame
of the black door is more black doors
of which there is only One

I see a black car under a
maple tree under a blue sky

The moon's almost invisible in
the blue sky

Each leaf stands out in the
clear air

Voices in the car are music
to the ears

41

The journey takes place and
before you know it you're
on it

What landscapes are flying out of
your eyes? What marketplaces
filled with hand-turned beads
and glass balls on strings! What
rainbow-colored things in stalls
like docile beasts waiting for
purchase!

And what sacred wells and ancient
trees planted in saintly places!

What darkness and light!

And then before you know it
the journey's end is in sight! Trumpets
in the distance! A lovely softness
to the edges of everything! All
signs pointing upward!

42

So when I die will I get
out of here like a slippery eel
or like a cranky antique
dealer who locks his doors for
fear someone might steal his
candelabras? This and that
thought pile up about this and that
and how it gets distributed or
destroyed

Words words words in books and
manuscripts derelict or headed
to good homes where there's a
warm reception and understanding

Do we leave rubble behind or
perhaps one polished brass
sphere that reflects the world
in its pure insubstantiality?

43

There are people all over the
world who stop periodically
every day to face God to thank
and praise and loosen the world's
hold on them and increase the
unseen splendor's attraction
for and to them all hopefully and
hopelessly for God's sake like
the waves of the sea do

and small creatures cleaning their
feelers and lions on hilltops
roaring and babies looking up at
their mothers full of trust and
love beyond their comprehension do

We pray like waves of the sea do

and God sees each wave as it
breaks and disappears

as we do

44

One day a Prince was
served a single tomato
when he was expecting a feast

His first reaction that poured
up through him was rage
until he saw that his rage
was the color of the tomato
only less bright and less
shiny

He looked again and while the
astonished courtiers held their
breath the Prince saw the tomato
transform into an angel of
brighter colors and greater shininess

who opened its wings that
extended from pole to pole
and polished the world

45

I've been in a house that
turned itself inside-out for
love of Allah and His Prophet
peace be upon him until there
was no room for anything but
love

The walls poured tears and the
floors prostrated the foreheads
of their boards in deeper submission

The tables groaned until a
feast was spread for the poor
and sheep were herded past its
chairs into courtyards of grace

So many angelic suspensions
rose that the roof
had to hold its breath until
the sky soothed its shingles
and peace descended

46

Even just a whispered breath
from the heart is enough as a
burnt offering in the ancient sense
and a pure offering in the
present tense

We look out from under eyes
that are lowered and bow
foreheads that are always in
prostration and our limbs from
head to toe shiver with God's
excitement

Then even the ocean senses these
seismic shifts and curls back
fringes of surf in acknowledgment

Even the fishes in the bottomless
dark passing each other with
neon headlamps know these
heartfelt whisperings for Allah

47

Ten minutes to the next
prayer and an earthquake
could blast the floor and walls

Nine minutes to the next prayer
and veils of light and darkness
could show Allah to Himself
through the eyes of our hearts

Eight minutes to the next prayer
and thoughts of our parents could
ease them in their graves

Seven minutes to the next prayer
and elephant infants could be born

Six minutes to the next prayer and
water could recede into the ground
everywhere

Five minutes to the next prayer and
suddenly Lover and Beloved are
One only and no second face is
ever possible anymore

48

Four minutes to the next prayer
and life bursts out in inane
conversations stray thoughts and
howling dogs asking God's
mercy for humankind

Three minutes to the next prayer and
a sudden convoy of angelic
trucks brings fresh water to
refugees in crowded camps

Two minutes to the next prayer
and forests become renewed with
great trees and bromiliads in bloom

One minute to the next prayer
and Azrael could appear facing
us directly and showing us the way
to Allah

The next prayer has come and we
stand in a row

as present as possible

49

Then the King can be seen as
a country groom among his
horses and sunlight coming in
through chinks in the barn

Don't be deceived

Push aside his leathern vest
and vestments of a rare
cloth studded with true star-
particles are revealed

When he rides off the sorrow of
his departure on the part of
the townspeople is palpable
and he leaves behind the living
chain of his sayings his
observations and his silences

No one can forget the sound
of hooves cantering away

50

Do the arrival and departure
of God's Friend have the same
impact?

Joy and expectation and grief
all at once? Nothing
remains as it was in their
precincts

What they know precedes
creation and remains long
after it dissolves

It's joy and expectation and grief
for ourselves both their
infinite loss and explosion unto Allah's
Magnificent Beauty rolling into
gorgeous sky and green
hills where before was only

a sameness under hidden
starlight

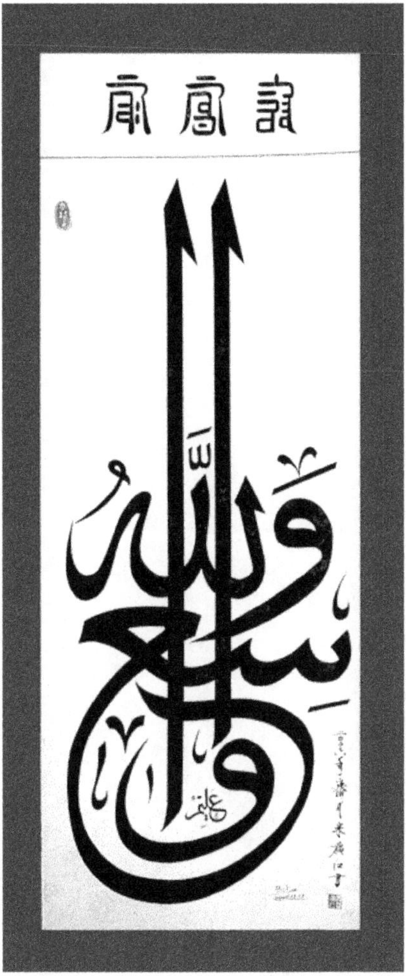

MYTHS WE NEVER KNEW

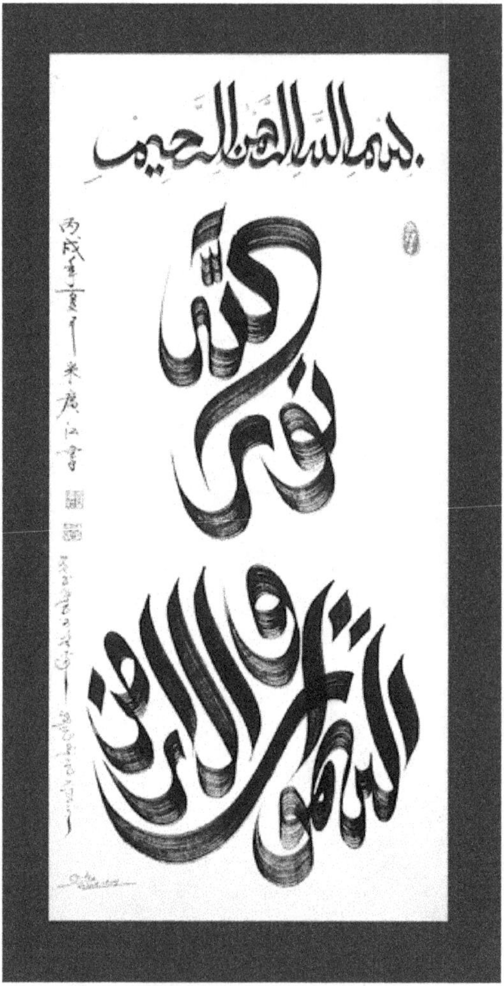
بسم الله الرحمن الرحيم

1

The stars used to be speckles on a dolphin's back
leaping through oceanic snow in sunlight

unseen by any but God

reflected in the mirrors of His ever-rolling waves
turned upside-down by time

2

Ever-rolling waves never look back

and never repeat themselves once they've
left the coil of their uncurling momentum

sliding across the aquatic dorsals of just
barely submerged leviathans

3

If we wonder where these arabesque thoughts
      come from
these caged beasts rattling the bars of their cages in
curious cadences

these front porches of words whose houses behind
      them
extend back to infinity

these emergences from silence whose famous cave
sometimes emits wisdom but most often among
      men
emits puffs of multi-colored smoke

And if we more attentively wonder where real
words of ever-rolling wisdom come from that
      astonish
any sensitive ears with the sterling of their silver
and the carats of their gold

we need only look with our hearts at how sunlight
      works
as it slides through every blade of grass to
warm the earth

or how soon babies learn to speak their fears and
    amazements

with mother-love tutoring and a few wrong moves
    corrected

Is it all the same swirl as ocean waves
whose energies come

from their own depths?

Whose eyes are always upon us
if not God's?

Whose ears hear everything?

Whose voice is the voice of the entire world?

Whose actions are all actions at once in every
    world and
all worlds at all times
everywhere?

A tiny glimpse may bring it all to bear

A soft whisper is enough to move mountains
and shake the air

4

Whales rose up to command the orbits
of great and small

significant and inconsequential

so that all things may have their
ends in their beginnings

their starts in their stops
pauses in continuations
sweetness in sour

God holding us to these things to see our faces
glow or glower

as all orbits make their serpent rounds
from car wheels to Saturn's rings turning

whales below in God's deeps below that
churning

5

That air around the earth is a spherical envelope
of angelic breathing

And when an airplane descends from flight slowly
down through clouds
it's all angel exhalations melodiously popping
in our ears

to get our rhythmic bearings

6

To get on with the threshing and plowing
The shaping and dissolving

The way waves crest and slide away
And clouds gather and sigh into nothingness

All it takes is a high heart
And eyes for beauty

And a silent mouth
And limbs that do God's work

In the back currents and forward flows
Into eternity and emptiness

Whose light dazzles and silence deafens
With its sweet amorous delicacies

7

We always wonder about death when it's
death that wonders about us

and why we are so oblivious to its charms
its whinnying stallions ready to take us to the

farthest horizon in its blaze of glory
or the firefly into the interior of its

flickering light

as night settles down over the land
letting its soft cloth down slowly so slowly

we barely notice the windows have gone
black and the rooms turned to silence

lips hands feet and shadows
dissolved into silent lips

but the eyes awake
on the other side

filled with delight

8

The doorway for all of us
is the same as for all of us

The little airplane of gold and dark chromium
dips its wings and we climb aboard

and out it goes through the
doorway for all of us

but the stairway to the doorway
is different for all of us

and the stairway on the
other side of the doorway

that leads down from that doorway

is how we are both before and
after that doorway

somewhere in the throat
somewhere in the heart

is different for all of us

how we do and how we are before we
get to the doorway

and who we are at the very moment when we
stand in that doorway before

going through

afloat or on our knees
and if we've been really on our knees

before we get to that
doorway

9

In simplicity is God's clarity
as if looking across a great prairie

directly into endless blue sky
in the heart and in the eye

of the eternal beholder
Who is Himself the Holder

of each tentacle and feeler
each sweet thought that steels

across the empty screen
that lies before after and between

each thing

TRANSLATION OF ARABIC CALLIGRAPHIES
(With thanks to Khalid and Manar Blankinship)

Title page: The *shahada*, or Islamic declaration of faith: *La ilaha illa Allah, Muhammad rasulullah,* There is no god but Allah, Muhammad is the Messenger of Allah.

Page 27: *Ya Rahman*, Oh Merciful!

Page 40: *Allahu Akbar*, Allah is Greater! (than anything conceivable)

Page 52 (and cover detail): The rose: The Divine Names with *Allah* at the center and on the petals, largest and second-largest, reading counter-clockwise: *Rahman*/Merciful, *Salaam*/Peaceful, *Raheem*/Compassionate, *Mumin*/Believer, *Malik*/Sovereign, *Muhaymin*/Protector, *Quddus*/Pure, *Aziz*/Mighty (etc. with Allah's Grace for the too-small-to-read petals). And at the bottom, from Qur'an, Surah 13/29: *'a-la bi-dhikr Allahi tatma' innu al-qulub*: "It is only by the remembrance of God that hearts are made tranquil."

Page 65: *Wa Allahu Wasi'u 'Alim*: And Allah is All-Encompassing, Knowing (Qur'an 2:247, etc.)

Page 68: *Allahu Nur al-samawati wa-al-ard*: Allah is the Light of the heavens and the earth (from Qur'an, Surah 24:35, etc.)

DANIEL ABDAL-HAYY MOORE

Born in 1940 in Oakland, California, Daniel Abdal-Hayy Moore had his first book of poems, *Dawn Visions*, published by Lawrence Ferlinghetti of City Lights Books, San Francisco, in 1964, and the second in 1972, *Burnt Heart/Ode to the War Dead*. He created and directed *The Floating Lotus Magic Opera Company* in Berkeley, California in the late 60s.

He became a Sufi Muslim in 1970, performed the Hajj in 1972, and lived and traveled throughout Morocco, Spain, Algeria and Nigeria, landing in California and publishing *The Desert is the Only Way Out,* and *Chronicles of Akhira* in the early 80s (Zilzal Press). Residing in Philadelphia since 1990, in 1996 he published *The Ramadan Sonnets* (Jusoor/City Lights), and in 2002, *The Blind Beekeeper* (Jusoor/Syracuse University Press). As of 2014, he has forty-two poetry titles in print with The Ecstatic Exchange.

He has been the major editor for a number of works, including *The Burdah* of Shaykh Busiri, translated by Shaykh Hamza Yusuf, and the poetry of Palestinian poet, Mahmoud Darwish, translated by Munir Akash. He is also widely published on the worldwide web, on his own website and poetry blog, among others: *www.danielmoorepoetry.com, www.ecstaticxchange.wordpress.com.* He was a winner of the Nazim Hikmet Prize poetry in 2011, 2012 and 2014, and in 2013 The American Book Award for *Blood Songs*, and was listed among the 500 Most Influential Muslims for his poetry.

HAJI NOOR DEEN MI GUANG JIANG

Haji Noor Deen Mi Guang Jiang is a renowned master of Arabic calligraphy. Born in 1963 in Shangdong province, China, he brings an immense learning in traditional thought and Islamic art to a modern audience, juxtaposing them in a new calligraphic style all his own, both Eastern and Western.

The Chinese and Arabic calligraphic traditions have often been compared as two of the world's finest manifestations of the written word, but never likened; indeed, they are at once opposites and complements. When combined the result is an artistic piece that is a work of incredibly unique beauty, and a testimony to man's synthesizing genius.

Noor Deen's extraordinary mastery and genius along with his unique ability to spectacularly deliver his craft to an audience has brought him lecture and workshop invitations from some of the most renowned and prestigious institutions around the world, including: Harvard University, Cambridge University, University of California-Berkley, Massachusetts Institute of Technology, the Bukhari Institute and many others. He currently lectures Arabic calligraphy at the Islamic College in Zhen Zhou, China and the Zaytuna Institute in California.

www.ingramcontent.com/pod-product-compliance
Lightning Source LLC
Chambersburg PA
CBHW062021040426
42447CB00010B/2093